Good Things Come in Small Packages!

Are you feeling sweet and sassy, like the Luscious Lemonade Cupcakes on page 16? Or are you the traditional type, like the Red Velvet Cupcakes found on page 36?

Maybe your perfect baby cake is as elegant and refined as a Meringue-Topped Raspberry Cupcake, as smooth and irresistible as a Brownie Peanut Butter Cupcake, or as rich and exotic as a Mandarin Coconut Delight.

Whether angelic or devilish, nutty or kissable, the cupcakes in this book will sweeten your days with plenty of pretty and delectable recipes to satisfy every desire. Go ahead and try them all. Then swap the cupcakes and toppings to make other perfect combinations. Perhaps there's more than one baby cake for you!

D0072542

Printed in the United States of America
by G&R Publishing Co.

Published By:

507 Industrial Street
Waverly, IA 50677

ISBN-13: 978-1-56383-334-2
ISBN-10: 1-56383-334-4
Item #7033

10 Cupcake-Making Tips

1. For best results, preheat the oven before baking cupcakes.

2. Grease muffin cups or small ramekins, or line each cup with paper or foil liners. Spoon the batter into prepared cups, filling each cup ½ to ⅔ full.

3. When baking a single pan of cupcakes, place the pan on the middle rack in the oven. Stagger multiple pans on racks so heat can circulate.

4. When a recipe calls for cake flour, do not use the self-rising type. If cake flour is not available, sift all-purpose flour, measure 1 cup and then remove 2 tablespoons; this will be equal to 1 cup of cake flour. For lighter cakes, add 2 tablespoons of corn starch to replace the 2 tablespoons of flour you removed. Sift again before using. (Make this in bulk and store it in an airtight container for future use. For example, combine 3½ cups flour and ½ cup cornstarch to make 4 cups of ready-to-use cake flour.)

5. Use your favorite cake recipes to make cupcakes. Prepare as directed, but spoon batter into baking cups. Bake at the same temperature as directed for cake, but shorten baking time by one-third to one-half. A recipe that makes a 2-layer cake will make 24 to 30 standard cupcakes.

6. If making miniature or jumbo cupcakes, adjust baking time accordingly. A recipe for 12 standard cupcakes will make about 30 miniature or 6 jumbo cupcakes.

7. Use the toothpick method to check the doneness on cupcakes made with butter, oil or shortening. A toothpick inserted in the center should come out clean when done. If the toothpick comes out wet, bake longer. For angel food, chiffon or sponge cupcakes, test doneness by touching tops lightly; they should spring back.

8. Try each cupcake recipe with other frostings and toppings in this book.

9. Refrigerate cupcakes frosted with dairy products such as cream cheese or whipping cream if they won't be eaten promptly.

10. Unfrosted cupcakes may be frozen in an airtight container and kept for several months. Thaw cupcakes before decorating.

Very Vanilla Cupcakes

Makes about 24 standard cupcakes

Cupcakes

2 large eggs
½ C. whole milk
½ tsp. vanilla extract
¾ C. plus 2 T. cake flour
½ C. plus 2 T. all-purpose flour

1 C. white sugar
1 T. baking powder
½ tsp. salt
½ C. unsalted butter, cut into cubes

White Drizzle Icing

2 C. powdered sugar
1 tsp. clear vanilla extract

3 to 4 T. milk
Colored candy sprinkles

Preparation

Preheat oven to 325°. Grease 24 muffin tin cups or fit the cups with paper liners.

In a large measuring cup, whisk together eggs, milk and vanilla; set aside. In a large mixing bowl, whisk together both flours, sugar, baking powder and salt. Add butter to bowl and use an electric mixer with paddles to mix until butter is coated with flour. By thirds, add egg mixture to bowl and beat at medium speed until ingredients are incorporated. Spoon batter evenly into the muffin cups.

Bake cupcakes for 17 to 20 minutes or until a toothpick inserted in the center comes out clean. Let the pans cool on a rack for 10 minutes before removing cupcakes from pans to cool completely.

Meanwhile, prepare the icing. Stir together powdered sugar, vanilla and enough milk to reach a thick drizzling consistency. Spread icing on cupcakes, allowing it to drizzle over edges. Immediately scatter sprinkles on top of wet icing.

Gingerbread Gal Cupcakes

Makes about 12 standard cupcakes

Cupcakes

1¼ C. all-purpose flour
1½ tsp. ground ginger
1 tsp. ground cinnamon
¼ tsp. ground cloves
½ tsp. ground allspice
¼ tsp. salt

¼ C. unsalted butter, softened
½ C. white sugar
½ C. unsulfured molasses
1 large egg, lightly beaten
1 tsp. baking soda
½ C. boiling water

Lemon Cream Cheese Frosting

8 oz. cream cheese, softened
2 T. unsalted butter, softened
1½ C. powdered sugar

½ tsp. vanilla extract
½ tsp. grated lemon zest
2 tsp. lemon juice

Preparation

Preheat oven to 350°. Grease 12 muffin tin cups or fit the cups with paper liners.

In a large bowl, whisk together the flour, ground spices and salt. In another bowl, cream together ¼ cup butter and sugar; beat until fluffy. Beat in molasses and egg until smooth. In a measuring cup, combine baking soda and boiling water, stirring until dissolved. Add baking soda mixture to molasses mixture, stirring well to combine. Stir molasses mixture into flour mixture until well combined. Spoon batter evenly into the muffin cups.

Bake the cupcakes for 20 minutes or until a toothpick inserted in the center comes out clean. Let the pan cool on a rack for 10 minutes before removing cupcakes from pan to cool completely.

Meanwhile, prepare the frosting. Cream together cream cheese and 2 tablespoons butter. Beat in remaining ingredients until fluffy and smooth. Chill frosting for 30 minutes. Pipe or spread frosting on cupcakes. Serve promptly or refrigerate.

Carrot Cupcakes

Makes about 12 standard cupcakes

Cupcakes

1 C. all-purpose flour
½ tsp. baking soda
½ tsp. baking powder
1 tsp. ground cinnamon
½ tsp. ground allspice
¼ tsp. salt

2 eggs
1 C. white sugar
½ C. vegetable oil
1½ C. grated carrots
¼ C. each chopped pecans, chopped raisins and sweetened flaked coconut, optional

Cream Cheese Frosting

4 oz. cream cheese, softened
2 T. unsalted butter, softened

¼ tsp. clear vanilla extract
1 C. powdered sugar
Mock Marzipan Carrots*

8

Preparation

Preheat oven to 325°. Grease 12 muffin tin cups or fit the cups with paper liners.

In a large bowl, whisk together the flour, baking soda, baking powder, ground spices and salt, set aside. In a separate mixing bowl, beat together eggs, sugar and oil. Gradually add flour mixture and blend well. Stir in carrots and optional nuts, raisins and coconut. Spoon batter evenly into the muffin cups.

Bake the cupcakes for 20 to 25 minutes or until a toothpick inserted in the center comes out clean. Let the pans cool on a rack for 5 minutes before removing cupcakes from pans to cool completely.

Meanwhile, prepare the frosting. Cream together cream cheese and butter. Beat in remaining ingredients until smooth. Spread frosting on cupcakes. Garnish with Mock Marzipan Carrots*, if desired. Serve promptly or refrigerate.

* Mix together 2 tablespoons white shortening, 1 tablespoon plus 1½ teaspoons water, 1 teaspoon almond extract and 2 cups powdered sugar. Knead until smooth and pliable. Divide into 2 portions. Wearing disposable gloves, knead orange food coloring into larger portion and green coloring into smaller portion. Form carrot and leaf shapes, adding details with a table knife. Dry slightly before placing on frosted cupcakes

Devilish Chocolate Cupcakes

Makes 24 standard cupcakes

Cupcakes

3 large eggs
1 C. mayonnaise
1 (18.25 oz.) box devil's food cake mix

1 C. water
2 tsp. vanilla extract

Chocolate Frosting

2 C. semi-sweet chocolate chips
1 C. sour cream
Chocolate Candy sprinkles,
  optional

Preparation

Preheat oven to 350°. Grease 24 muffin tin cups or fit the cups with paper liners.

In a large mixing bowl, beat eggs. Beat in mayonnaise. Add cake mix, water and vanilla, mixing until well combined. Spoon batter evenly into the muffin cups.

Bake the cupcakes for 25 minutes or until a toothpick inserted in the center comes out clean. Let the pans cool on a rack for 10 minutes before removing cupcakes from pans to cool completely.

Meanwhile, prepare the frosting. Melt chocolate chips in the microwave for 60 seconds; stir and repeat until smooth. Whisk in sour cream. Pipe or spread frosting on cupcakes immediately and decorate tops with chocolate sprinkles, if desired.

Milky Way Sweetcakes

Makes about 18 standard cupcakes

Cupcakes

10 miniature Milky Way candy bars, unwrapped and chopped

¼ C. butter

1 C. white sugar

½ C. shortening

2 medium eggs

1¼ C. all-purpose flour

½ tsp. salt

¾ C. buttermilk

¼ tsp. baking soda

½ tsp. vanilla extract

Toppings

1 (16 oz.) can ready-to-spread
  chocolate frosting
Miniature semi-sweet
  chocolate chips

Chopped pecans
Caramel ice cream topping
Milk chocolate kiss candies,
  unwrapped

Preparation

Preheat oven to 350°. Grease 18 muffin tin cups or fit the cups with paper liners.

In a heavy saucepan over low heat, melt candy bars and butter, stirring until smooth; set aside. In a large mixing bowl, beat together sugar and shortening until creamy. Add eggs, beating just until blended; set aside. In a separate bowl, combine flour and salt; set aside. In a measuring cup, stir together buttermilk and baking soda. Gradually add flour and buttermilk mixtures alternately to sugar mixture. Beat at low speed after each addition, just until blended. Stir in melted candy bar mixture and vanilla. Spoon batter evenly into the muffin cups.

Bake the cupcakes for 18 minutes or until a toothpick inserted in the center comes out clean. Let the pans cool on a rack for 10 minutes before removing cupcakes from pans to cool completely.

Spread frosting on cupcakes. Sprinkle some chocolate chips and pecans on top. Drizzle with caramel topping. Add a piped dollop of frosting in the center and top with a chocolate kiss.

Carnival Poke Cupcakes

Makes about 24 standard cupcakes

Cupcakes

1 (18.25 oz.) box plain white cake mix

Eggs, oil and water as directed on box

1 (3 oz.) pkg. gelatin, any color or flavor

1 C. boiling water

14

Toppings

4 C. powdered sugar
½ C. butter, melted
1 T. clear vanilla extract

4 to 5 T. half & half
Food coloring
Additional powdered sugar

Preparation

Preheat oven to 350°. Grease 24 muffin tin cups or line the cups with paper liners.

In a large mixing bowl, combine cake mix with eggs, oil and water as directed on cake mix box. Mix as directed and spoon batter evenly into the muffin cups.

Bake as directed for cupcakes. Let the pans cool on a rack for 10 minutes. Meanwhile, place dry gelatin mix in a bowl and add boiling water; stir until dissolved and set aside. Pierce top of each cupcake several times with a fork. Spoon gelatin mixture over cupcakes. Refrigerate for 30 minutes.

Meanwhile, prepare the toppings. Combine 4 cups powdered sugar, butter, vanilla and enough half & half to make a thick drizzling consistency. Frost cupcakes with a smooth layer of icing, reserving ¾ cup icing. Divide reserved icing among four bowls; tint each with food coloring. Stir additional powdered sugar into each bowl to reach piping consistency. Transfer colored icings into separate plastic freezer bags, cut off a corner of each bag and pipe lines of icing on cupcakes as desired.

15

Luscious Lemonade Cupcakes

Makes about 30 standard cupcakes

Cupcakes

1 (6 oz.) can frozen lemonade concentrate, thawed

1 (18.25 oz.) box white cake mix

1 (8 oz.) carton sour cream

1 (3 oz.) pkg. cream cheese, softened

3 large eggs

Pink Lemonade Buttercream Frosting

½ C. vegetable shortening
½ C. butter, softened
2 to 3 T. lemon juice or remaining lemonade concentrate
1 tsp. grated lemon zest

4 C. powdered sugar
Additional lemon juice
Pink food coloring
Candied lemon slices or drops, optional

Preparation

Preheat oven to 350°. Grease 30 muffin tin cups or fit the cups with paper liners.

Remove 2 tablespoons of lemonade concentrate from can and reserve for frosting or another use. In a large mixing bowl, combine remaining concentrate, cake mix, sour cream, cream cheese and eggs; beat at low speed until moistened. Beat at high speed for 3 minutes. Spoon batter evenly into the muffin cups.

Bake the cupcakes for 22 minutes or until a toothpick inserted in the center comes out clean. Let the pans cool on a rack for 10 minutes before removing cupcakes from pans to cool completely.

Meanwhile, prepare the frosting. Cream together shortening and butter. Beat in 2 tablespoons lemon juice and zest. Add powdered sugar gradually and beat until light and fluffy, adding food coloring and additional lemon juice if needed. Frost cupcakes and garnish with candied lemon slices or drops.

Marshmallow Surprise Cupcakes

Makes about 16 standard cupcakes

Cupcakes

¾ C. butter, softened
1½ C. white sugar
2 large eggs
2 C. all-purpose flour

½ C. unsweetened cocoa powder
2 tsp. baking powder
½ tsp. salt
1 C. milk
1 (7 oz.) jar marshmallow creme

18

Glossy Chocolate Icing

¾ C. heavy whipping cream
3 T. unsalted butter
1½ T. light corn syrup

9 oz. bittersweet and/or semi-sweet chocolate, chopped
1½ T. kirsch or vanilla extract

Preparation

Preheat oven to 350°. Grease 16 muffin tin cups or fit the cups with paper liners.

In a large mixing bowl, cream together ¾ cup butter and sugar until smooth. Add eggs and beat well. In a separate bowl, whisk together flour, cocoa powder, baking powder and salt. Stir half of flour mixture into butter mixture. Stir in milk until blended. Mix in remaining flour mixture. Spoon batter evenly into the muffin cups, until almost full.

Bake the cupcakes for 20 minutes or until a toothpick inserted in the center comes out clean. Let the pans cool on a rack for 5 minutes before removing cupcakes from pans to cool completely.

Spoon marshmallow creme into a pastry bag with a ½" round tip. Insert tip into the top of cupcakes and squeeze some filling into each one.

In a medium saucepan, simmer whipping cream, 3 tablespoons butter and corn syrup. Reduce heat, add chocolate and stir until melted. Mix in kirsch and remove from heat. Let stand 1 hour to cool and thicken; stir several times. Spread icing on cupcakes. Refrigerate leftovers.

Mint Melt-Aways

Makes about 24 standard cupcakes

Cupcakes

1 (18.25 oz.) box chocolate fudge cake mix with pudding

Eggs, oil and water as directed on box

½ tsp. peppermint flavoring

1 C. mint or crème de menthe baking chips

Mint Frosting

1 (3 oz.) pkg. cream cheese,
   softened
¼ C. butter, softened
4 C. powdered sugar
3 T. milk

1 tsp. vanilla extract
¼ tsp. peppermint flavoring
Green food coloring
Milk chocolate candy bar, shaved

Preparation

Preheat oven to 350°. Grease 24 muffin tin cups or fit the cups with paper liners.

In a large mixing bowl, combine cake mix with eggs, oil and water as directed on cake mix box. Beat for 2 minutes on medium speed. Stir in ½ teaspoon peppermint flavoring and baking chips. Spoon batter evenly into the muffin cups.

Bake the cupcakes for 21 to 26 minutes or until a toothpick inserted in the center comes out clean. Let the pans cool on a rack for 10 minutes before removing cupcakes from pans to cool completely.

Meanwhile, prepare the frosting. Cream together cream cheese and butter. Gradually beat in half of powdered sugar. Stir in milk, vanilla, ¼ teaspoon peppermint flavoring and food coloring. Beat in remaining powdered sugar until smooth.

Spread frosting on cupcakes. Garnish with chocolate shavings. Serve promptly or refrigerate.

Angelic Cupcakes

Makes about 24 cupcakes

Cupcakes

½ C. sifted cake flour

¾ C. white sugar, divided

6 large egg whites, room temperature

½ tsp. cream of tartar

⅛ tsp. salt

1 tsp. vanilla extract

¾ tsp. lemon juice

22

Fluffy White Frosting

2 large egg whites, room
   temperature
1½ C. white sugar
Dash of salt

⅓ C. cold water
2 tsp. light corn syrup
1 tsp. vanilla extract
Fresh blueberries

Preparation

Preheat oven to 325°. Fit 24 muffin tin cups with paper liners.

In a small bowl, whisk together flour and 6 tablespoons sugar; set
aside. In a large mixing bowl, beat egg whites until frothy. Add cream
of tartar and salt; beat until soft peaks form. Gradually add remaining
6 tablespoons sugar and beat until stiff peaks form. Beat in vanilla and
lemon juice. Sift half of flour mixture over egg white mixture; fold in.
Repeat with remaining flour mixture until blended. Spoon batter evenly
into the muffin cups.

Bake the cupcakes for 15 minutes or until they spring back when lightly
touched. Let the pans cool on a rack for 5 minutes before removing
cupcakes from pans to cool completely.

Meanwhile, prepare the frosting. In the top of a double boiler, combine
all ingredients except vanilla and blueberries. Beat with an electric
mixer to blend, then set pan over boiling water. Beat for 7 minutes
or until stiff peaks form. Remove from water, add vanilla and beat to
spreading consistency, about 2 minutes. Spread frosting on cupcakes.
Garnish with blueberries.

23

Scrumptious Strawberry Cupcakes

Makes about 24 standard cupcakes

Cupcakes

2½ C. cake flour

1 tsp. baking soda

¼ tsp. salt

½ C. unsalted butter, softened

1½ C. white sugar

2 large eggs

⅓ C. buttermilk

¼ C. canola oil

1 tsp. vanilla extract

1 C. finely chopped fresh or frozen strawberries

24

Strawberry Frosting

1 C. butter
3½ C. powdered sugar
½ tsp. vanilla extract

½ C. frozen strawberries, thawed
 and pureed
Fresh strawberries

Preparation

Preheat oven to 350°. Grease 24 muffin tin cups or fit the cups with paper liners.

In a medium bowl, whisk together flour, baking soda and salt; set aside. In a large mixing bowl, cream together butter and sugar. Add eggs, beating until smooth and creamy. Mix in buttermilk, oil and vanilla until well combined. Blend flour mixture into butter mixture, just until combined. Gently stir in 1 cup strawberries. Spoon batter evenly into the muffin cups.

Bake the cupcakes for 18 to 20 minutes or until a toothpick inserted in the center comes out clean. Let the pans cool on a rack for 10 minutes before removing cupcakes from pans to cool completely.

Meanwhile, prepare the frosting. Cream together butter and salt until light and fluffy. Slowly add powdered sugar, beating until well mixed. Blend in vanilla and 3 tablespoons of pureed strawberries until creamy. Reserve any remaining puree for another use. Spread frosting on cupcakes. Garnish with strawberry slices.

Mandarin Coconut Delights

Makes about 12 standard cupcakes

Cupcakes

1½ C. all-purpose flour

1½ tsp. baking powder

½ tsp. baking soda

½ tsp. salt

½ C. white sugar

⅓ C. vegetable oil

1 egg

½ C. orange juice

½ C. mandarin oranges, drained

½ C. vanilla or white chocolate chips

26

Orange Buttercream Frosting

⅓ C. butter, softened
2 C. powdered sugar
Pinch of salt

1 tsp. grated orange zest, optional
2 T. orange juice
Coconut Topping*

Preparation

Preheat oven to 375°. Grease 12 muffin tin cups or fit the cups with paper liners.

In a large bowl, whisk together flour, baking powder, baking soda and salt; set aside. In a separate bowl, combine the sugar, oil, egg and ½ cup orange juice; mix well. Add dry ingredients to orange juice mixture and stir just until moistened. Fold in oranges and vanilla chips. Spoon batter evenly into the muffin cups.

Bake the cupcakes for 15 to 20 minutes or until a toothpick inserted in the center comes out clean. Let the pan cool on a rack for 10 minutes before removing cupcakes from pan to cool completely.

Meanwhile, prepare the frosting. Beat together butter, powdered sugar, salt, zest and 2 tablespoons orange juice until smooth. Frost cupcakes and sprinkle with Coconut Topping.

> * In a skillet, melt 1 tablespoon butter. Stir in ½ cup sweetened flaked coconut and 3 tablespoons white sugar. Toast until golden brown, stirring often; let cool.

Orange Kiss-Me Cupcakes

Makes about 18 standard cupcakes

Cupcakes

2 large eggs, separated
⅛ tsp. cream of tartar
½ C. butter, softened
1 C. sugar

1 tsp. vanilla extract or orange flavoring
1¾ C. cake flour
½ tsp. salt
2½ tsp. baking powder
½ C. orange juice

28

Orange Frosting

3 T. butter, softened
1½ C. powdered sugar
⅛ tsp. salt

1 T. grated orange zest
2 to 3 T. orange juice
Candied Orange Zest Strips*

Preparation

Preheat oven to 350°. Grease 18 muffin tin cups or fit the cups with paper liners.

In a small mixing bowl, beat egg whites until frothy. Add cream of tartar and beat until stiff peaks form; set aside. In a medium mixing bowl, cream together butter, sugar, egg yolks and vanilla until smooth. In a separate bowl, whisk together flour, salt and baking powder. By thirds, add flour mixture and orange juice alternately to creamed mixture. Fold in beaten egg whites. Spoon batter evenly into the muffin cups.

Bake the cupcakes for 15 minutes or until a toothpick inserted in the center comes out clean. Let the pan cool on a rack for 10 minutes before removing cupcakes from pan to cool completely.

Meanwhile, prepare the frosting. Beat together all ingredients except zest strips until smooth, using enough orange juice to reach desired consistency. Spread frosting on cupcakes. Garnish with Candied Orange Zest Strips.

* Peel thin strips of orange zest from 2 oranges. Simmer strips in water for 6 minutes; drain. Combine cup water and cup sugar in saucepan and simmer strips for 15 minutes. Remove strips, cool slightly and roll in sugar. Cool completely before use.

29

Pretty in Pink Cupcakes

Makes about 24 standard cupcakes

Cupcakes

1 (18.25 oz.) box white cake mix with pudding

1¼ C. buttermilk

¼ C. butter, melted

2 large eggs

2 tsp. vanilla extract

½ tsp. almond extract

30

White Decorator Frosting

½ C. white shortening
2 C. powdered sugar
½ tsp. clear vanilla extract
1½ tsp. meringue powder

¼ tsp. salt
2 to 3 T. water
Pink shaved candy*

Preparation

Preheat oven to 350°. Grease 24 muffin tin cups or fit the cups with paper liners.

In a large mixing bowl, combine cake mix, buttermilk, melted butter, eggs and both extracts; mix until blended. Increase speed and beat 2 minutes or until batter is smooth. Spoon batter evenly into the muffin cups.

Bake the cupcakes for 25 minutes or until a toothpick inserted in the center comes out clean. Let the pans cool on a rack for 10 minutes before removing cupcakes from pans to cool completely.

Meanwhile, prepare the frosting. Beat together shortening, powdered sugar, vanilla, meringue powder and salt until smooth. Beat in enough water to reach desired consistency. Spread frosting on cupcakes. Sprinkle shaved candy over frosting, pressing it down gently.

* Melt ½ cup pink candy wafers in the microwave; stir until smooth. Pour onto waxed paper and spread into a thin rectangle. Place in freezer for 2 minutes or until set. With a vegetable peeler, shave off thin ribbons of candy from one edge.

Nutty Banana-Maple Cupcakes

Makes about 16 standard cupcakes

Cupcakes

1 (14 oz.) box banana quick bread mix

1 C. buttermilk

¼ C. vegetable oil

3 T. maple syrup

½ tsp. vanilla extract

2 large eggs

½ C. finely chopped walnuts

Maple Cream Cheese Frosting

4 oz. cream cheese, softened
2 T. butter, softened
3 T. maple syrup
½ tsp. vanilla extract

½ tsp. maple flavoring
2 C. powdered sugar
16 walnut halves

Preparation

Preheat oven to 400°. Grease 16 muffin tin cups or fit the cups with paper liners.

In a large bowl, combine bread mix, buttermilk, oil, 3 tablespoons syrup, vanilla and eggs, stirring 50 to 75 strokes or until moistened. Stir in chopped walnuts until well blended. Spoon batter evenly into the muffin cups.

Bake the cupcakes for 16 to 20 minutes or until a toothpick inserted in the center comes out clean. Let the pans cool on a rack for 5 minutes before removing cupcakes from pans to cool completely.

Meanwhile, prepare the frosting. In a small mixing bowl, beat together cream cheese, butter, 3 tablespoons syrup, vanilla and maple flavoring until smooth. Gradually add powdered sugar and beat to reach desired consistency. Spread frosting on cupcakes and place a walnut half on top. Serve promptly or refrigerate.

Sweetheart Chocolate Cupcakes

Makes about 14 standard cupcakes

Cupcakes

½ C. butter, softened

1 C. white sugar

1 egg

1 tsp. vanilla extract

1½ C. all-purpose flour

½ C. unsweetened cocoa powder

1 tsp. baking soda

¼ tsp. salt

½ C. buttermilk

½ C. strong brewed coffee
  or warm water

Chocolate Frosting & Candy Toppers

2¾ C. powdered sugar
6 T. unsweetened cocoa powder
6 T. butter, softened
4 to 6 T. evaporated milk

1 tsp. vanilla extract
Crushed toffee
Chocolate covered heart candies
Ready-to-use red icing in a tube

Preparation

Preheat oven to 350°. Grease 14 muffin tin cups or fit the cups with paper liners.

In a small mixing bowl, cream together butter and sugar. Beat in egg and 1 teaspoon vanilla. In a separate bowl, whisk together flour, ½ cup cocoa powder, baking soda and salt. Add flour mixture, buttermilk and coffee alternately to creamed mixture. Spoon batter evenly into the muffin cups.

Bake the cupcakes for 25 to 30 minutes or until a toothpick inserted in the center comes out clean. Let the pans cool on a rack for 10 minutes before removing cupcakes from pans to cool completely.

Meanwhile, prepare the frosting. Whisk together powdered sugar and 6 tablespoons cocoa powder; set aside. Cream butter; add powdered sugar mixture and milk alternately to butter and beat to reach desired consistency. Stir in 1 teaspoon vanilla.

Spread frosting on cupcakes. Dust with toffee and set a chocolate candy on top. Drizzle with red icing; let dry before serving.

Traditional Red Velvet Cupcakes

Makes about 24 standard cupcakes

Cupcakes

½ C. unsalted butter, softened

1½ C. white sugar

2 large eggs

3 T. unsweetened cocoa powder

2 T. red food coloring (more if desired)

2½ C. all-purpose flour

1 tsp. salt

1 C. buttermilk

1 tsp. vanilla extract

¼ C. water

1 tsp. cider vinegar

1 tsp. baking soda

Cream Cheese Frosting

1 (8 oz.) pkg. cream cheese,
  softened
½ C. unsalted butter, softened

1½ C. powdered sugar
1 tsp. clear vanilla extract
Tiny white nonpareils, optional

Preparation

Preheat oven to 350°. Grease 24 muffin tin cups or fit the cups with paper liners.

In a large mixing bowl, cream together ½ cup butter and sugar until fluffy. Beat in eggs. In a small bowl, make a paste of cocoa powder and food coloring; blend into creamed mixture. In a separate bowl, whisk together flour and salt; add to creamed mixture and mix well. Beat in buttermilk, vanilla and water. In a small bowl, combine vinegar and baking soda; fold vinegar mixture into cake batter just until blended. Spoon batter evenly into the muffin cups.

Bake the cupcakes for 15 to 20 minutes or until a toothpick inserted in the center comes out clean. Let the pans cool on a rack for 10 minutes before removing cupcakes from pans to cool completely.

Meanwhile, prepare the frosting. Beat together cream cheese, ½ cup butter, powdered sugar and vanilla until smooth and creamy. Spread frosting on cupcakes. Sprinkle with nonpareils, if desired. Serve promptly or refrigerate.

Out of the Blue Coconut Snowballs

Makes about 20 standard cupcakes

Cupcakes

1 (18.25 oz.) box plain white cake mix

1⅓ C. coconut milk or whole milk

2 T. vegetable oil

3 eggs

2 tsp. coconut flavoring

38

Whipped Cream & Coconut Topping

1 (7 oz.) bag sweetened flaked
   coconut
Blue food coloring

1 C. heavy whipping cream
2 T. powdered sugar
Candy sprinkles, optional

Preparation

Preheat oven to 350°. Grease 20 muffin tin cups or fit the cups with paper liners. Place a small mixing bowl and beaters in the freezer to chill.

In a large mixing bowl, combine cake mix, milk, oil, eggs and coconut flavoring; beat until blended. Increase speed and beat for 2 minutes until well mixed. Spoon batter evenly into the muffin cups.

Bake the cupcakes for 18 to 22 minutes or until cupcakes spring back when lightly touched. Let the pans cool on a rack for 10 minutes before removing cupcakes from pans to cool completely.

Meanwhile, prepare the toppings. Place coconut in a zippered plastic bag. Add food coloring, seal bag and incorporate color by shaking and kneading bag. Spread colored coconut on a plate to dry slightly before use. Using the chilled bowl and beaters, whip the cream until slightly thickened. Gradually add sugar, beating just until soft peaks form. Do not overbeat. Spread whipped cream on cupcakes. Sprinkle generously with coconut, pressing it down gently. Serve promptly or refrigerate.

39

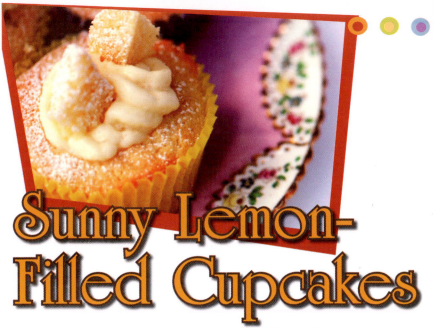

Sunny Lemon-Filled Cupcakes

Makes about 18 standard cupcakes

Cupcakes

2 C. cake flour

1¼ C. white sugar, divided

2 tsp. baking powder

1 (3 oz.) pkg. lemon gelatin

¾ C. milk

⅔ C. vegetable oil

2 T. lemon flavoring

3 eggs, separated

Lemon Filling

1 (3 oz.) pkg. French vanilla
  instant pudding mix
1½ C. milk

1 tsp. lemon flavoring
Powdered sugar

Preparation

Preheat oven to 325°. Grease 18 muffin tin cups or fit the cups with paper liners.

In a large mixing bowl, stir together flour, 1 cup sugar, baking powder and gelatin powder. Add milk, oil and lemon flavoring, mixing well. Beat in egg yolks, one at a time. In a separate small mixing bowl, beat egg whites until stiff, gradually adding remaining ¼ cup sugar. Fold beaten egg whites into batter until well combined. Spoon batter evenly into the muffin cups.

Bake cupcakes for 20 to 25 minutes or until a toothpick inserted in the center comes out clean. Let the pans cool on a rack for 10 minutes before removing cupcakes from pans to cool completely.

Meanwhile, prepare the filling. Whisk together pudding mix, milk and lemon flavoring until smooth and thick. Cut out and remove a cylinder of cake from the center of each cupcake. Pipe lemon filling into the opening, allowing some filling to mound out. Use removed pieces of cake to garnish cupcake tops and sprinkle with powdered sugar. Serve promptly or refrigerate.

41

Merry Margarita Cupcakes

Makes about 24 standard cupcakes

Cupcakes

1 (18.25 oz.) box plain white
  cake mix

1 (10 oz.) can frozen Margarita mix
  (like Bacardi), thawed

3 egg whites

2 T. vegetable oil

1 T. grated lime zest

42

Toppings

2 C. ready-to-spread vanilla
  frosting

1 tsp. grated lime zest

Fresh or candied lime slices

Preparation

Preheat oven to 350°. Grease 24 muffin tin cups or fit the cups with paper liners.

In a large mixing bowl, combine cake mix, Margarita mix, egg whites and oil. Beat for 1 to 2 minutes until well mixed. Stir in 1 tablespoon lime zest until blended. Spoon batter evenly into the muffin cups.

Bake the cupcakes for 22 to 24 minutes or until a toothpick inserted in the center comes out clean. Let the pans cool on a rack for 10 minutes before removing cupcakes from pans to cool completely.

Meanwhile, prepare the toppings. Combine frosting and 1 teaspoon lime zest, stirring until well mixed. Spread frosting on cupcakes and garnish each cupcake with a lime slice.

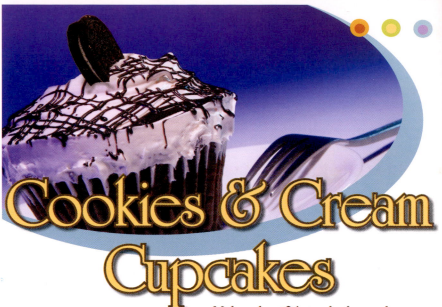

Cookies & Cream Cupcakes

Makes about 24 standard cupcakes

Cupcakes

1 (18.25 oz.) box plain chocolate cake mix

Eggs, oil and water as directed on box

1 (8 oz.) pkg. cream cheese, softened

1 egg

2 T. white sugar

24 bite size Oreo chocolate sandwich cookies

Toppings

2 C. whipped topping, thawed
Chocolate syrup

24 bite size Oreo chocolate
sandwich cookies

Preparation

Preheat oven to 350°. Grease 24 muffin tin cups or fit the cups with paper liners.

In large mixing bowl, combine cake mix with eggs, oil and water as directed on cake mix box; set aside. In a medium bowl, stir together cream cheese with egg and sugar until smooth and well mixed. Spoon a portion of the cake batter into the muffin cups, filling each cup no more than ½ full. Top batter with about 1½ teaspoons cream cheese mixture and 1 cookie. Use remaining cake batter to evenly cover the filling in each cupcake.

Bake cupcakes for 19 to 22 minutes or until a toothpick inserted in the center comes out clean. Let the pans cool on a rack for 10 minutes before removing cupcakes from pans to cool completely.

Just before serving, spread whipped topping over cupcakes. Drizzle with chocolate syrup and set a cookie on top.

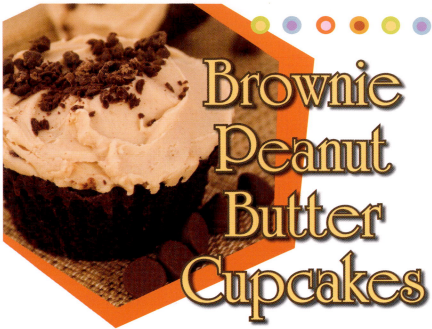

Brownie Peanut Butter Cupcakes

Makes about 18 standard cupcakes

Cupcakes

1 (19.5) oz. box traditional fudge brownie mix

½ C. vegetable oil

¼ C. water

2 large eggs

1 C. semi-sweet chocolate chips

Peanut Butter Frosting

1 (16 oz.) can ready-to-spread
  vanilla frosting
¾ C. creamy peanut butter

Chocolate sprinkles or chopped
  chocolate chips, optional

Preparation

Preheat oven to 350°. Grease 18 muffin tin cups or fit the cups with paper liners.

In a medium bowl, combine brownie mix, oil, water and eggs, stirring until well blended. Spoon batter evenly into the muffin cups. Place a spoonful of chocolate chips in the center of batter.

Bake cupcakes for 18 to 20 minutes or until set. Let the pans cool on a rack for 10 minutes before removing cupcakes from pans to cool completely.

Meanwhile, prepare the frosting. Stir together the vanilla frosting and peanut butter until smooth. Spread frosting on cupcakes and garnish with chocolate sprinkles.

Chocolate Cherry Cupcakes

Makes about 24 standard cupcakes

Cupcakes

1 (18.25 oz.) plain devil's food
   cake mix

2 T. unsweetened cocoa powder

1⅓ C. buttermilk

½ C. vegetable oil

3 large eggs

1 tsp. cherry flavoring

⅓ C. finely chopped maraschino
   cherries, well-drained, optional

Cherry Buttercream Frosting

⅓ C. butter, softened
3 C. powdered sugar
1½ tsp. cherry flavoring
2 to 3 T. milk

Red food coloring, optional
Milk chocolate candy bars, shaved
24 whole maraschino cherries with
   stems, well-drained

Preparation

Preheat oven to 350°. Grease 24 muffin tin cups or fit the cups with paper liners.

In a large mixing bowl, combine the cake mix, cocoa powder, buttermilk, oil, eggs and cherry flavoring. Blend until moistened, then increase speed and beat for 2 minutes more until well mixed. Fold in chopped cherries, if desired. Spoon batter evenly into the muffin cups.

Bake the cupcakes for 16 to 20 minutes or until a toothpick inserted in the center comes out clean. Let the pans cool on a rack for 10 minutes before removing cupcakes from pans to cool completely.

Meanwhile, prepare the frosting. Cream together butter and powdered sugar. Beat in cherry flavoring, milk and food coloring to reach desired consistency and color. Spread frosting on cupcakes, sprinkle with chocolate shavings and place a cherry on top.

49

Cappuccino Cupcakes

Makes about 24 standard cupcakes

Cupcakes

1 (18.25 oz.) box plain yellow
  cake mix

Eggs, oil and water as directed
  on box

2 T. instant coffee powder

50

Cappuccino Frosting

2 T. instant coffee powder

2 tsp. hot water

1 (16 oz.) can ready-to-spread
  cream cheese frosting

Milk chocolate candy wafers
  (such as Make 'n Mold) or kisses

Preparation

Preheat oven to 350°. Grease 24 muffin tin cups or fit the cups with
paper liners.

In a large mixing bowl, combine cake mix, eggs, oil and water as
directed on cake mix box, dissolving 2 tablespoons of coffee powder in
the water before combining. Mix as directed. Spoon batter evenly into
the muffin cups.

Bake the cupcakes for 18 to 20 minutes or until a toothpick inserted in
the center comes out clean. Let the pans cool on a rack for 10 minutes
before removing cupcakes from pans to cool completely.

Meanwhile, prepare the frosting. Dissolve 2 tablespoons coffee powder
in hot water. Stir coffee mixture into frosting until smooth and well
blended. Spread frosting on cupcakes and garnish with chocolate
wafers. Serve promptly or refrigerate.

Sponge Cake Cupcakes

Makes about 18 standard cupcakes

Cupcakes

6 large eggs, separated

2 T. ice water

¼ tsp. cream of tartar

1 C. white sugar

1 C. cake flour

¼ tsp. salt

1 tsp. lemon juice

¼ tsp. almond extract

Whipped Cream Topping

1 C. heavy whipping cream
2 to 3 T. white sugar

1½ tsp. almond extract
Fresh strawberries

Preparation

Preheat oven to 325°. Fit 18 muffin tin cups with paper liners. Place a small mixing bowl and beaters in the freezer to chill.

In a medium mixing bowl, combine egg yolks and ice water; set aside. In a large mixing bowl, beat egg whites until frothy. Add cream of tartar and beat until stiff; set aside. Beat egg yolks until lemon-colored. Add sugar and beat until blended. In a separate bowl, whisk together flour and salt. Fold flour mixture into egg yolk mixture, a third at a time, until fully incorporated. Stir in lemon juice and ¼ teaspoon extract. Fold egg yolk mixture into the stiff egg whites until blended. Spoon batter evenly into the muffin cups.

Bake the cupcakes for 20 to 25 minutes or until cupcakes spring back when lightly touched. Let cupcakes cool completely in the pans.

Meanwhile, prepare the whipped topping. Using the chilled bowl and beaters, whip the cream until slightly thickened. Gradually beat in 2 to 3 tablespoons sugar and 1½ teaspoons extract, until soft peaks form. Just before serving, pipe topping on cupcakes and garnish with strawberries.

Spiced Pumpkin Cupcakes

Makes about 24 standard cupcakes

Cupcakes

2 C. all-purpose flour

1 (3.4 oz.) pkg. butterscotch instant pudding mix

2 tsp. baking soda

¼ tsp. salt

1 T. ground cinnamon

½ tsp. ground ginger

½ tsp. ground allspice

¼ tsp. ground cloves

1 C. butter, softened

1 C. white sugar

1 C. brown sugar

4 eggs

1 tsp. vanilla extract

1 (15 oz.) can pumpkin puree

54

Topping

Mock Marzipan Pumpkins
(see recipe on page 9)

2 C. prepared cream cheese
frosting (use recipe on page 9
or a ready-to-spread frosting)

Ground cinnamon

Preparation

Preheat oven to 350°. Grease 24 muffin tin cups or fit the cups with paper liners.

In a medium bowl, whisk together flour, pudding mix, baking soda, salt and ground spices; set aside. In a large mixing bowl, beat together butter and both sugars until light and fluffy. Add eggs, one at a time, beating well after each addition. Beat in vanilla and pumpkin puree. Stir in flour mixture just until blended. Spoon batter evenly into the muffin cups.

Bake the cupcakes for 20 minutes or until a toothpick inserted in the center comes out clean. Let the pans cool on a rack for 10 minutes before removing cupcakes from pans to cool completely.

Meanwhile, follow the directions on page 9 to make Mock Marzipan Pumpkins. Attach green stems to pumpkins with light pressure; let dry. Frost cupcakes, sprinkle with cinnamon and garnish with pumpkins if desired. Serve promptly or refrigerate.

Meringue-Topped Raspberry Cupcakes

Makes about 12 standard cupcakes

Cupcakes

1½ C. all-purpose flour
1½ tsp. baking powder
¼ tsp. salt
½ C. butter, softened
¾ C. white sugar

1 large egg
2 egg yolks
3 T. raspberry juice blend
1½ tsp. vanilla extract
½ C. milk

Meringue

4 large egg whites at room temperature
¼ tsp. cream of tartar

⅔ C. white sugar
12 fresh raspberries, optional

Preparation

Preheat oven to 350°. Grease 12 muffin tin cups or fit the cups with paper liners.

In a small bowl, whisk together flour, baking powder and salt; set aside. In a large mixing bowl, cream butter; add ¾ cup sugar and beat well. Add egg, egg yolks, liqueur and vanilla; beat until well combined. Add flour mixture and milk alternately to creamed mixture, beating after each addition until blended. Spoon batter evenly into the muffin cups.

Bake the cupcakes for 15 minutes. Meanwhile, prepare meringue. Wash beaters thoroughly. Beat egg whites until frothy. Add cream of tartar and beat until soft peaks form. Gradually add ⅔ cup sugar, beating well until stiff peaks form.

Spread meringue on top of partially-baked cupcakes and gently press a raspberry on top of each one, if desired. Return to oven to bake for 8 to 10 minutes or until meringue is lightly browned. Let the pan cool on a rack for 5 minutes before removing cupcakes from the pan. Serve warm, or cover loosely and chill before serving.

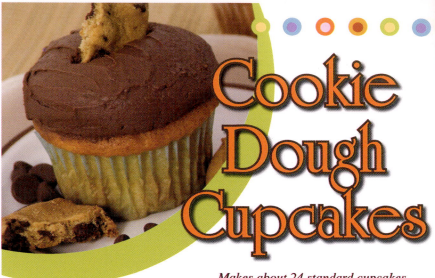

Cookie Dough Cupcakes

Makes about 24 standard cupcakes

Cupcakes

1 (18.25 oz.) box plain yellow cake mix

1 (3.4 oz.) vanilla instant pudding mix

1 C. whole milk

1 C. vegetable oil

4 large eggs

1 tsp. vanilla extract

Refrigerated chocolate chip cookie dough, cut into 24 small pieces and frozen

58

Chocolate Buttercream Frosting

½ C. butter, softened
½ C. unsweetened cocoa powder
3 C. powdered sugar
1 tsp. vanilla extract
3 to 5 T. milk or half & half
Mini chocolate chip cookies

Preparation

Preheat oven to 350°. Grease 24 muffin tin cups or fit the cups with paper liners.

In a large mixing bowl, combine cake mix, pudding mix, milk, oil, eggs and vanilla. Blend until moistened, then increase speed and beat for 2 minutes more until well mixed. Spoon batter evenly into the muffin cups. Place one piece of frozen cookie dough on top of batter in each cup.

Bake the cupcakes for 23 to 27 minutes or until cupcakes spring back when lightly touched. Let the pans cool on a rack for 5 minutes before removing cupcakes from pans to cool for 15 minutes more. The centers may sink down.

Meanwhile, prepare the frosting. Cream together butter and cocoa powder. Add powdered sugar, vanilla and 3 tablespoons of milk, beating on low speed until well blended. Increase speed and beat until light and fluffy, adding more milk to reach desired consistency. Spread or pipe frosting on slightly warm cupcakes and garnish with cookies.

Metric Conversion Chart

Abbreviations

C. = cup	qt. = quart	mL = milliliter
T. = tablespoon	gal. = gallon	F = Fahrenheit
tsp. = teaspoon	lb. = pound	C = Celsius
oz. = ounce	g = gram	
pt. = pint	L = liter	

Weights (mass)

½ oz.	15 g
1 oz.	30 g
3 oz.	90 g
4 oz.	120 g
8 oz.	225 g
10 oz.	285 g
12 oz.	360 g
16 oz. (1 lb.)	450 g

Oven Temperatures

250°F	120°C
275°F	140°C
300°F	150°C
325°F	160°C
350°F	180°C
375°F	190°C
400°F	200°C
425°F	220°C
450°F	230°C

Baking Pan Sizes

Pan Size	Size (in/ qt)	Metric Volume	Size (cm)
Baking or Cake Pan (square or rectangle)	8 x 8 x 2	2 L	20 x 20 x 5
	9 x 9 x 2	2.5 L	23 x 23 x 5
	8 x 12 x 2	3 L	30 x 20 x 5
	9 x 13 x 2	3.5 L	33 x 23 x 5
Loaf Pan	4 x 8 x 3	1.5 L	20 x 10 x 7
	5 x 9 x 3	2 L	23 x 13 x 7
Round Layer Cake Pan	8 x 1½	1.2 L	20 x 4
	9 x 1½	1.5 L	23 x 4
Pie Plate	8 x 1¼	750 mL	20 x 3
	9 x 1¼	1 L	23 x 3
Baking Dish or Casserole	1 quart	1 L	–
	1½ quart	1.5 L	–
	2 quart	2 L	–

Volume Measurements (dry)

⅛ tsp.	0.5 mL
¼ tsp.	1 mL
½ tsp.	2 mL
¾ tsp.	4 mL
1 tsp.	5 mL
1 T.	15 mL
2 T.	30 mL
¼ C.	60 mL
⅓ C.	75 mL
½ C.	125 mL
¾ C.	175 mL
1 C.	250 mL
2 C. (1 pt.)	500 mL
3 C.	750 mL
4 C. (1 qt.)	1 L

Volume Measurements (fluid)

1 fluid oz. (2 T.)	30 mL
4 fluid oz. (½ C.)	125 mL
8 fluid oz. (1 C.)	250 mL
12 fluid oz. (1½ C.)	375 mL
16 fluid oz. (2 C.)	500 mL

Dimensions

1/16 inch	2 mm
⅛ inch	3 mm
¼ inch	6 mm
½ inch	1.5 cm
¾ inch	2 cm
1 inch	2.5 cm